LOST IN
The Wilds of Canada

JOHN CADIZ

M&S

For Monica

CANADIAN CATALOGUING IN PUBLICATION DATA

Cadiz, John
   Lost in the wilds of canada

ISBN 0-7710-1828-2

1. National characteristics, Canadian – Caricatures and cartoons. 2. Canada – Social life and customs – Caricatures and cartoons. 3. Canadian wit and humor, Pictorial. I. Title.

NC1449.C33A4 1997   741'971   C97-931147-0

The publishers acknowledge the support of the Canada Council for the Arts and the Ontario Arts Council for their publishing program.

Printed and bound in Canada.

McClelland & Stewart Inc.
The Canadian Publishers
481 University Avenue
Toronto, Ontario
M5G 2E9

1 2 3 4 5 01 11 99 98 97

SQUEEGEE BEARS

URBAN PESTS

LODGE MEETINGS

WHEN THE BLACKFLIES RETURN

EARLY RADIO COLLARS

ANIMAL TRAPPERS

CROSS DRESSING IN THE WILDS

BIGLOOS ~ MONSTER HOMES OF THE ARCTIC

THE AURORA BORING-ALIS

THE FAILURE OF CANADA'S FIRST GATED COMMUNITY

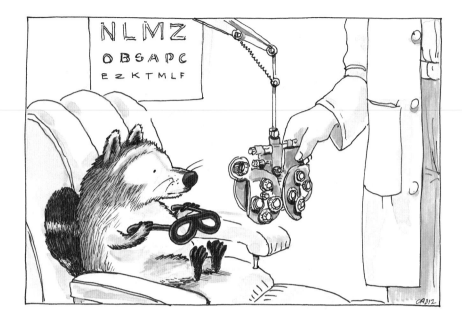

CONRAD BLACK BUYS ANOTHER NEWSPAPER.

THE TROUBLE WITH OTTER PILOTS

THE ANNUAL HOUSE HUNT

YOU BE THE JUDGE

THE STREET HOCKEY FINALS

A DAY AT THE RACES

THE HUNCHBACK OF BEAVER DAM

ELVIS STOJKO SCORES AT HIS DAY JOB

CANADA'S DONOVAN BAILEY FINALLY CONCEDES DEFEAT

THE ANNUAL HUSKY ROUNDUP

THE AMAZING POWER OF THE CANADIAN FLAG IN FOREIGN LANDS

SIGNS OF SPRING

ELEPHANTS OF THE ARCTIC

FINALLY, PROOF THAT CANADA
WAS SECOND CHOICE FOR
EARLY IMMIGRANTS